Up to 30-minute recipes: Mediterranean diet

Longevity book

by Olivia Efso

Hello! Let's get acquainted!

I am Olivia Efso. I am a mother, a wife, and just a simple woman, but what sets me apart is my passion for a healthy lifestyle and the desire to be useful in this life!
It is no secret that nutrition plays a major role in our lives, and its responsibility falls on women's shoulders in most cases. I am no exception, and I am very happy about it!
I love to cook and find inspiration and pleasure in it.

I hope that my experience and expertise in this will be useful to people. In this regard, I am very excited to bring you this diet cookbook, which I use every day myself.

Of the many diets, I chose the Mediterranean diet for myself and my loved ones. I cannot help but agree with the statement of Dr. Ramón Estruch, a prominent Spanish physician and researcher widely recognized for his groundbreaking work on the Mediterranean diet and its impact on health and longevity: "The Mediterranean diet is more than just a diet; it is a way of living that encompasses healthy eating, physical activity, and social interactions. It is this holistic approach that makes the Mediterranean diet so beneficial for health and longevity.".

In this book, you will find dishes that are universal for everyone. Additionally, I offer you 3 free bonuses to easily understand the concept of the Mediterranean lifestyle for your well-being.

My dishes are easy to cook: up to 30 minutes without losing quality and benefits, and only about 5 ingredients that are available a step away from you or one click online. I followed these principles when creating my recipes.

Time-saving is the main concept of my book, so that you can leave more time for yourself, your family, and friends for other things you like to do and activities. I think we can all agree that so often we lack this for happiness.

Trust me, my recipes are incredibly tasty and simple, and I can't wait for you to try each one of them. As soon as you do, please let me know how you like it! I welcome all feedback, so please do not be shy.

I wish you all health and longevity!
Enjoy your meal!
All the Best!

Yours, Olivia Efso

COPYRIGHT © 2024 OLIVIA EFSO. ALL RIGHTS RESERVED.

No part of this document may be reproduced, duplicated, or transmitted in any form, whether electronic or printed, without the written permission of the publisher. Recording of this publication is strictly prohibited, and any storage of this document is not allowed without the publisher's written consent — all rights reserved.

The information provided herein is stated to be accurate and consistent. Any liability related to the use or misuse of any policies, processes, or directions contained within is solely and entirely the responsibility of the recipient reader. Under no circumstances will the publisher be held legally responsible for any reparations, damages, or monetary loss arising from the information herein, whether directly or indirectly.

Copyrights for materials not held by the publisher remain with the respective authors. The information provided is for informational purposes only and is universally applicable as such. The presentation of the information is made without any contract or guarantee.

Trademarks used are without consent, and the publication of trademarks is without permission or endorsement from the trademark owner. All trademarks and brands mentioned in this book are used solely for illustrative purposes and are owned by their respective owners, not affiliated with this document.

DISCLAIMER

The information provided in this Mediterranean diet cookbook is intended for educational purposes only and is not a replacement for professional medical advice, diagnosis, or treatment. While Mediterranean diets are widely recognized for their health benefits, individual dietary needs can vary significantly. Always consult with a healthcare provider, registered dietitian, or nutritionist before making any changes to your diet, especially if you have health conditions or dietary restrictions.

The recipes and nutritional information in this book are based on general guidelines for a balanced Mediterranean diet, which includes an emphasis on fruits, vegetables, whole grains, lean proteins, and healthy fats. However, these recommendations may not be suitable for everyone. Personal health goals, allergies, and intolerances should be considered when planning your meals.

The author and publisher do not accept responsibility for any adverse effects or consequences resulting from the use of the recipes or information contained within this book. Any reliance on the content is at your own risk. Always seek professional advice tailored to your individual health needs before implementing new dietary practices.

CONTENT

About This Book	5
Mediterranean Diet Guide	6
Cooking Conversions (special bonus)	7
Breakfast	8
Lunch	24
Dinner	40
Salads	56
Desserts	64
Beverages	72
Shopping list (special bonus)	80
Week meal plan	80
Weight Management	83
Let's stay in touch (special bonus)	84

ABOUT THIS BOOK

With great joy and love, I want to offer you my view on health and longevity in everyday nutrition! The Mediterranean Diet is more than just a way of eating; it is a holistic approach to longevity and healthy life, that prioritizes simplicity, quality, and natural foods. Throughout this cookbook, including all bonuses, you'll find detailed explanations, tips, and insights that will help you understand the philosophy behind the diet, targeted to longevity and healthy life, as well as the science that supports its benefits. All recipes are crafted with local ingredients in mind, available a step away from you or a click away online, making it easier to source what you need and enjoy meals that are both familiar and new.

Each recipe uses **up to 5 ingredients** and is designed **to be prepared in 30 minutes or less**. This is the main concept of this book so that you can leave more time for yourself, and always remain active.

By following the structured **4(+) -week meal plan** laid out in these pages and supporting this knowledge with a friendly budget interactive shopping list, you'll be able to reach your victories, ensuring a sustainable and rewarding result.

Specifically for the residents accustomed to the metric system of measurement I've included a conversion chart for weight and volume measurements to help you easily navigate the recipes.
This will assist you in understanding the quantities and making adjustments as needed. Each recipe includes nutritional information, with approximate values for each serving. Inside, you will be able to get a bonus covering the principles of the Mediterranean diet for longevity in the form of a mini book and recipes for breakfasts, lunches, and dinners, all tailored for **two servings**. As additional care, I've included recipes for salads, desserts, and drinks to complement your meals.

The Mediterranean diet allows for flexibility, encouraging you to tailor the flavors to your personal preference. Feel free to use any of your favorite spices and salt in the recipes, adjusting the amounts to your taste. The key is to adhere to the core principles of the Mediterranean diet, such as using **fresh vegetables, whole grains, and healthy fats**, which nature has generously gifted us with.

The **images*** of the dishes are just one possible presentation. If your results look a little different, that's perfectly okay. The most important thing is to enjoy the process, experiment with new flavors, and strive for a healthier lifestyle through delicious and nutritious food.

Whether you're starting or looking to refine your approach, this book is your ultimate companion on the longevity diet journey, designed to guide you through one of the healthiest and most delicious ways to eat.

*AI-assisted

MEDITERRANEAN DIET GUIDE

In Mediterranean countries like Greece, Italy, Spain, southern France, Monako, and Cyprus, ancient culinary habits are deeply rooted in the Mediterranean diet, which is more than just a pattern of eating. This diet emphasizes fresh, unprocessed foods and encourages a well-rounded approach to nutrition. It is well-known for its ability to lengthen life and improve health.

10 Key Principles

1. Fruits and vegetables: A person's basic diet should contain a variety of fresh fruits and vegetables. They supply vital vitamins, minerals, and antioxidants.

2. Select Only Complete Grains: Make sure to include whole wheat bread, brown rice, and oats among your options. These help maintain stable blood sugar levels and sustained, long-lasting feelings of fullness.

3. Olive Oil: The main source of fat, olive oil is well-known for having a high concentration of heart-healthy monounsaturated fats. Lipids not only promote cardiovascular health but also have anti-inflammatory qualities.

4. Balanced Protein Consumption: Make fish your primary protein source because it's high in heart-healthy omega-3 fatty acids. Reduce red meat and swap it out for leaner proteins like chicken or turkey.

5. Dairy Products: It's recommended to consume dairy products in moderation, with an emphasis on items like cheese and yogurt. Choose reduced-fat options if you're trying to lose weight.

6. Plant-Based Proteins: Make sure that foods like kidney or black beans, green peas, and chickpeas are your main sources of plant-based protein. Because they are rich in fiber, vitamins, and minerals, these legumes provide a fantastic alternative to red meat.

7. Nuts and Seeds: Packed with healthy fats, fiber, and protein, nuts and seeds are a great addition to any diet. They increase your metabolism and help you feel fuller longer.

8. Herbal Teas and Fresh Fruit Beverages: You can substitute herbal teas and fresh fruit beverages for alcohol. These options offer vitamins and antioxidants, making them healthy and refreshing alternatives without the risks associated with alcohol consumption.

9. Drink A Lot of Water: Make water your go-to beverage to ensure you keep properly hydrated all day. Prioritize drinking water over other beverages.

10. Physical Activity: Frequent exercise is a crucial component of the Mediterranean diet. Exercises that enhance general health and well-being include cycling, swimming, and walking.

The traditional diet in the Mediterranean has always been based on foods that were easily cultivated or gathered in the region. Olive groves, vineyards, and wheat fields dominated the agricultural landscape, creating the foundation for daily meals. Bread, olive oil, and wine—three key elements that became symbols of the Mediterranean diet—were not just food staples but also a part of the region's cultural and religious heritage. Fishing also played a significant role, and fish, along with other seafood, became a primary source of protein in the region.

Medical journals and magazines make us aware of the importance of nutrients in daily meals for maintaining our longevity and active form. **If you are interested in a new scientific justification for the benefits of the Mediterranean diet, I suggest you take my first special digital mini bonus. Don't worry, your private data will be safe!**

To collect a bonus, **scan this QR code with your smartphone** to get access immediately and without any obligations!

FIRST SPECIAL BONUS IS HERE

COOKING CONVERSIONS: GRAMS, OUNCES, AND CUPS

Conversion Table for Dry Ingredients

Measurment	oz	g
1 teaspoon	0.15 oz	~5 g
1 tablespoon	0.5 oz	~15 g
1/8 cup	1 oz	~28 g
1/4 cup	2 oz	~56 g
1/3 cup	2.7 oz	~75 g
1/2 cup	4 oz	~113 g
1 cup	8 oz	~226 g
1 1/2 cup	12 oz	~340 g
2 cup	16 oz	~450 g
4 cup	32 oz	~900 g

Conversion Table for Liquids

Measurment	fl oz	ml
1 teaspoon	0.2 fl oz	~5 ml
1 tablespoon	0.5 fl oz	~15 ml
1/8 cup	1 fl oz	~30 ml
1/4 cup	2 fl oz	~60 ml
1/3 cup	2.7 fl oz	~80 ml
1/2 cup	4 fl oz	~120 ml
1 cup	8 fl oz	~240 ml
1 1/2 cup	12 fl oz	~350 ml
2 cup	16 fl oz	~470 ml
4 cup	32 fl oz	~950 ml

BREAKFAST

Breakfast plays an essential role in the Mediterranean diet, laying a healthy foundation for the rest of the day. It's important because it replenishes the body's energy and nutrients after hours of fasting overnight. A typical Mediterranean breakfast might include whole grains, fresh fruits, nuts, and yogurt, which provide a good mix of fiber, protein, and vitamins. By focusing on natural, minimally processed foods in the morning, you support heart health and boost your metabolism, helping you stay energized throughout the day. Starting your day with a balanced breakfast not only gives you a positive start but also supports your overall well-being in the long run.

Muesli with Almond Milk and Fruit

Ingredients:

1/2 cup of muesli
1 cup of almond milk
1/2 of banana, sliced
1/4 cup of fresh raspberries
1/4 cup of fresh blueberries

Nutritional Information:
(per serving)

Calories: ~290 kcal
Protein: ~6 g
Fat: ~8 g
Carbs: ~52 g
Sugar: ~18 g
Fiber: ~7 g

Instructions:

1. In a bowl, mix muesli with almond milk and let it sit for 5 minutes to soften.
2. Add banana and berries, stir and serve.

Whole Grain Toast with Tomatoes

Ingredients:

2 whole grain toasts
2 medium chopped tomatoes
1/2 cup of feta cheese
2 teaspoons of olive oil
spices and fresh herbs

Nutritional Information:
(per serving)

Calories: ~250 kcal
Protein: ~8 g
Fat: ~14 g
Carbs: ~28 g
Sugar: ~4 g
Fiber: ~5 g

Instructions:

1. Spread the toast with olive oil.
2. Top with tomatoes and feta.
3. Add spices and fresh herbs to your taste.

Oatmeal with Berries and Almonds

Ingredients:

1 cup of rolled oats
2 cups of almond milk
1/2 cup of fresh blueberry
1/2 cup of fresh raspberry
2 tablespoons of almonds

Nutritional Information:
(per serving)

Calories: ~300 kcal
Protein: ~7 g
Fat: ~10 g
Carbs: ~45 g
Sugar: ~8 g
Fiber: ~6 g

Instructions:

1. In a saucepan, bring the milk to a boil.
2. Add the oats and cook for 5-7 minutes until tender.
3. Transfer to a bowl, and add berries and almonds.

Greek Yogurt with Fruit and Chia Seeds

Ingredients:

2 cups of greek yogurt
1/2 cup of chopped fruits (apples, pears)
1/2 cup of berries (blueberries, raspberries)
2 tablespoons of chia seeds
fresh mint

Nutritional Information:
(per serving)

Calories: ~280 kcal
Protein: ~14 g
Fat: ~9 g
Carbs: ~35 g
Sugar: ~20 g
Fiber: ~8 g

Instructions:

1. Mix yogurt and chia seeds in a bowl. Let sit for 20 minutes.
2. Add chopped fruits and berries to the bowl.

Spinach and Tomato Omelet

Ingredients:
4 eggs
1 cup of fresh spinach
2 medium chopped tomatoes
2 tablespoons olive oil
spices and fresh herbs

Nutritional Information:
(per serving)
Calories: ~300 kcal
Protein: ~14 g
Fat: ~22 g
Carbs: ~8 g
Sugar: ~4 g
Fiber: ~2 g

Instructions:
1. Heat the oil in a skillet.
2. Whisk the eggs, add spinach and tomatoes.
3. Pour the mixture into the skillet and cook until done.

Whole Grain Pancakes with Honey

Ingredients:

1 cup of whole grain flour
2 eggs
1 cup of almond milk
2 tablespoons of honey
1/2 cup of berries and nuts

Nutritional Information:
(per serving)

Calories: ~280 kcal
Protein: ~10 g
Fat: ~8 g
Carbs: ~40 g
Sugar: ~12 g
Fiber: ~5 g

Instructions:

1. Mix whole grain flour, eggs and almond milk until smooth.
2. Cook pancakes on a skillet until golden brown on both sides.
3. Drizzle with honey and serve with berries and nuts.

Avocado Toast with Poached Egg

Ingredients:

2 whole grain toasts
1 large avocado
1 tablespoon of olive oil
2 eggs
spices and fresh herbs

Nutritional Information:
(per serving)

Calories: ~280 kcal
Protein: ~12 g
Fat: ~18 g
Carbs: ~22 g
Sugar: ~1 g
Fiber: ~7 g

Instructions:

1. Mash the avocado with olive oil and spread it on the toast.
2. Prepare a poached egg (or soft-boil) and place it on the toast.

Oatmeal with Kiwi and Chia Seeds

Ingredients:
1 cup of rolled oats
2 cups of almond milk or water
2 kiwi fruits, peeled and sliced
2 tablespoons of chia seeds
1 tablespoon of honey

Nutritional Information:
(per serving)

Calories: ~260 kcal
Protein: ~7 g
Fat: ~7 g
Carbs: ~44 g
Sugar: ~12 g
Fiber: ~8 g

Instructions:

1. Bring almond milk or water to a boil, add rolled oats, and cook for 5-7 minutes until done.
2. Stir in diced kiwi, chia seeds, and honey. Mix well and serve.

Bruschetta with Tomatoes and Basil

Ingredients:

4 slices of whole grain baguette
1 cup of chopped tomatoes
1 tablespoon of olive oil
1 garlic clove
fresh basil leaves

Nutritional Information:
(per serving)

Calories: ~200 kcal
Protein: ~5 g
Fat: ~10 g
Carbs: ~25 g
Sugar: ~3 g
Fiber: ~3 g

Instructions:

1. Toast baguette slices on the grill, in a frying pan or in a toaster.
2. Rub each slice with the garlic clove.
3. Mix the chopped tomatoes with olive oil, salt, and pepper. Top the baguette with the tomato mixture and garnish with basil leaves.

Eggs with Avocado and Tomatoes

Ingredients:

4 eggs
1 medium avocado
1 medium chopped tomato
2 tablespoons of olive oil
spices and fresh herbs

Nutritional Information:
(per serving)

Calories: ~300 kcal
Protein: ~14 g
Fat: ~24 g
Carbs: ~8 g
Sugar: ~3 g
Fiber: ~6 g

Instructions:

1. Fry the eggs in olive oil.
2. Slice the avocado and tomatoes.
3. Place the eggs on a plate and add the avocado and tomatoes.
4. Add spices and herbs to your taste

Quinoa with Nuts and Honey

Ingredients:

1 cup of quinoa
2 cups of water
2 tablespoons of honey
1 cup of nuts (almonds, cashews)
fresh mint

Nutritional Information:
(per serving)

Calories: ~280 kcal
Protein: ~8 g
Fat: ~12 g
Carbs: ~35 g
Sugar: ~10 g
Fiber: ~5 g

Instructions:

1. Rinse quinoa, bring to a boil with water, and cook for 15-20 minutes.
2. Transfer to a bowl, add honey and nuts.

Tuna and Avocado Toast

Ingredients:

2 whole grain toasts
1 medium avocado
1/2 cup of canned tuna
1 teaspoon of lemon juice
spices and fresh herbs

Nutritional Information:
(per serving)

Calories: ~300 kcal
Protein: ~18 g
Fat: ~18 g
Carbs: ~20 g
Sugar: ~1 g
Fiber: ~5 g

Instructions:

1. Mash the avocado and spread it on the toast.
2. Mix the tuna with lemon juice, salt, and pepper, and place on top.
3. Add spices and herbs to your taste.

Vegetable and Feta Cheese Frittata

Ingredients:

4 eggs
1/2 cup of chopped tomatoes
1/2 cup of spinach
1/2 cup of chopped mushrooms
1/2 cup of feta cheese

Nutritional Information:
(per serving)

Calories: ~320 kcal
Protein: ~18 g
Fat: ~24 g
Carbs: ~6 g
Sugar: ~2 g
Fiber: ~2 g

Instructions:

1. Beat the eggs and add chopped vegetables and feta.
2. Heat olive oil in a pan and pour the egg mixture in.
3. Cook on medium heat until done.

Toast with Hummus and Vegetables

Ingredients:

2 whole grain toasts
1/2 cup of hummus
1 small chopped cucumber
1 small chopped bell pepper
spices and fresh herbs

Nutritional Information:
(per serving)

Calories: ~220 kcal
Protein: ~8 g
Fat: ~10 g
Carbs: ~25 g
Sugar: ~3 g
Fiber: ~5 g

Instructions:

1. Spread hummus on the toast.
2. Top with chopped vegetables.
3. Add spices and herbs to your taste.

Broccoli and Parmesan Omelet

Ingredients:

6 eggs
1 cup of chopped broccoli
4 tablespoons of Parmesan cheese
2 tablespoons of olive oil
spices and fresh herbs

Nutritional Information:
(per serving)

Calories: ~320 kcal
Protein: ~20 g
Fat: ~22 g
Carbs: ~10 g
Sugar: ~2 g
Fiber: ~2 g

Instructions:

1. Sauté the broccoli in olive oil until tender.
2. Beat the eggs and pour them over the broccoli.
3. Sprinkle with grated Parmesan and cook over medium heat until set.
4. Add spices and herbs to your taste.

LUNCH

　　Lunch is an integral part of the Mediterranean diet, providing a balanced, nutritious break during the day. It typically features a variety of fresh vegetables, whole grains, lean proteins like fish or poultry, and healthy fats from olive oil or nuts. This combination offers essential nutrients and keeps energy levels stable throughout the afternoon. Mediterranean lunches often include dishes like salads with olive oil dressing, whole-grain wraps, or legumes, which are rich in fiber and promote digestive health. By focusing on wholesome, minimally processed ingredients, lunch supports heart health, maintains steady blood sugar levels, and sustains overall vitality and well-being.

Fish with Garlic and Brussel Sprouts

Ingredients:

12 oz of fish fillet (cod, seabass)
1 cup of halved brussels sprouts
2 minced garlic cloves
2 tablespoons of olive oil
1 teaspoon of lemon juice and wedges

Nutritional Information:
(per serving)

Calories: ~330 kcal
Protein: ~28 g
Fat: ~18 g
Carbs: ~12 g
Sugar: ~3 g
Fiber: ~5 g

Instructions:

1. Cook the garlic and Brussels sprouts, stirring, for 10-15 minutes until soft. Season with salt and pepper to taste. Transfer to a plate.
2. Add oil to the same pan. Add the fish, salt and pepper, lemon juice, and cook for 5-7 minutes on each side.
3. Serve the fish with the Brussels sprouts and a lemon wedge.

Chickpea Soup with Tomatoes

Ingredients:

1 cup of drained canned chickpeas
1 cup of diced tomatoes
1/2 cup of diced onion
1 minced garlic clove
2 tablespoons olive oil

Nutritional Information:
(per serving)

Calories: ~300 kcal
Protein: ~15 g
Fat: ~10 g
Carbs: ~35 g
Sugar: ~6 g
Fiber: ~8 g

Instructions:

1. In a pot, heat olive oil and sauté onion and garlic until soft. Add tomatoes, and cook for 5 minutes.
3. Add chickpeas and 2 cups of water, add salt and spices (cumin is especially suitable here) to taste, bring to a boil and simmer for 15 minutes.

Pasta with Tomato Olive Sauce

Ingredients:

1 cup of whole-grain pasta (spaghetti)
1/2 cup of tomato sauce
1/2 cup of olives
1/2 cup of grated parmesan cheese
2 tablespoons of olive oil

Nutritional Information:
(per serving)

Calories: ~400 kcal
Protein: ~12 g
Fat: ~15 g
Carbs: ~55 g
Sugar: ~8 g
Fiber: ~6 g

Instructions:

1. Cook pasta according to package instructions. It usually takes 10-15 minutes.
2. In a pan, heat olive oil, add tomato sauce and olives, and cook for 5-7 minutes. Add salt and spices to taste. Toss sauce with pasta.
4. Sprinkle the finished dish with parmesan cheese and serve.

Vegetable Stew

Ingredients:

1 cup of diced eggplant
1 cup of diced zucchini
1 cup of diced tomatoes
1/2 cup of diced onion
2 tablespoons of olive oil

Nutritional Information:
(per serving)

Calories: ~250 kcal
Protein: ~5 g
Fat: ~15 g
Carbs: ~30 g
Sugar: ~10 g
Fiber: ~8 g

Instructions:

1. Heat olive oil in a pan. Sauté onion until soft.
2. Add eggplant, zucchini, and tomatoes. Add salt and spices to taste.
3. Cook for 20 minutes under the lid.

Rice with Vegetables and Feta

Ingredients:

1 cup of cooked brown rice (or long grain & wild rice pilaf)
1 cup of chopped bell peppers
1 cup of chopped zucchini
1/2 cup of feta cheese
2 tablespoons of olive oil

Nutritional Information:
(per serving)

Calories: ~400 kcal
Protein: ~12 g
Fat: ~14 g
Carbs: ~60 g
Sugar: ~8 g
Fiber: ~8 g

Instructions:

1. Bring water to a boil, add rice, reduce heat, and simmer for 25 minutes until cooked.
2. Along with this, in a skillet, heat olive oil and sauté vegetables until tender (about 10-15 minutes). Season with salt and pepper.
3. Mix the cooked rice with the vegetables, add feta, and toss.

Tomato Basil Soup

Ingredients:

2 cups of tomato juice
1 cup of finely chopped onion
2 cloves of minced garlic
1/2 cup of chopped fresh basil
2 tablespoons of olive oil

Nutritional Information:
(per serving)

Calories: ~200 kcal
Protein: ~5 g
Fat: ~10 g
Carbs: ~25 g
Sugar: ~10 g
Fiber: ~4 g

Instructions:

1. In a pot, heat olive oil and sauté onion and garlic until soft.
2. Add tomato juice and bring to a boil. Simmer for 10 minutes.
3. Add basil and add salt and spices to taste. Can be served with croutons.

Pasta with Mushrooms and Parmesan

Ingredients:

2 cups of whole-grain pasta (fettuccine)
1 cup of sliced mushrooms
2 cloves of minced garlic
1/4 cup of grated Parmesan cheese
2 tablespoons of olive oil

Nutritional Information:
(per serving)

Calories: ~400 kcal
Protein: ~12 g
Fat: ~16 g
Carbs: ~50 g
Sugar: ~6 g
Fiber: ~6 g

Instructions:

1. Cook fettuccine according to package instructions (~7-10 minutes).
2. In a skillet, heat olive oil and sauté garlic until golden. Add mushrooms and cook until tender 7-10 minutes. Mix it all.
3. Sprinkle with Parmesan. Season with salt, pepper, and fresh herbs.

Chicken Vegetable Rice

Ingredients:

1 cup of cooked brown rice
7 oz of diced chicken breast
1/2 cup of diced carrot
1/2 cup of drained canned green peas
2 tablespoons of olive oil

Nutritional Information:
(per serving)

Calories: ~400 kcal
Protein: ~25 g
Fat: ~15 g
Carbs: ~50 g
Sugar: ~5 g
Fiber: ~7 g

Instructions:

1. Bring water to a boil, add rice, reduce heat, and simmer for 25 minutes until cooked.
2. Along with this, sauté chicken in olive oil until cooked for 10 minutes. Add vegetables and cook until tender 10 minutes.
3. Mix with cooked rice and season with salt and spices to taste.

Salmon with Broccolis

Ingredients:

10 oz of salmon
1 cup of chopped broccoli
2 tablespoons of olive oil
1 sliced lemon
a sprig of rosemary

Nutritional Information:
(per serving)

Calories: ~400 kcal
Protein: ~30 g
Fat: ~25 g
Carbs: ~15 g
Sugar: ~8 g
Fiber: ~6 g

Instructions:

1. Preheat oven to 200°C (400°F).
2. Place salmon and vegetables on a baking sheet, drizzle with olive oil and place lemon wedges next to the salmon. Add salt and spices to taste, a sprig of rosemary.
3. Bake for 20-25 minutes.

Lavash with Hummus and Vegetables

Ingredients:

2 lavashes (or tortillas)
1 cup of hummus
1/2 cup of sliced cucumbers
1/2 cup of sliced tomatoes
2 tablespoons of olive oil

Nutritional Information:
(per serving)

Calories: ~350 kcal
Protein: ~10 g
Fat: ~15 g
Carbs: ~45 g
Sugar: ~5 g
Fiber: ~8 g

Instructions:

1. Spread hummus on the lavash.
2. Top with vegetables. Add olive oil, salt and spices to taste.
3. Roll up the lavash.
3. Dress with olive oil and vinegar.

Boiled Potatoes with Green Beans

Ingredients:

1 cup of diced potatoes
1 cup of boiled green beans
1/2 cup of diced red onion
2 tablespoons of olive oil
1 tablespoon of vinegar

Nutritional Information:
(per serving)

Calories: ~300 kcal
Protein: ~8 g
Fat: ~15 g
Carbs: ~35 g
Sugar: ~5 g
Fiber: ~7 g

Instructions:

1. Boil potatoes for 20-25 minutes. At the same time, boil green beans for 5-10 minutes. Let it cool a little.
2. In a bowl, mix potatoes, green beans, and red onion. Add salt and spices to taste.
3. Dress with olive oil and vinegar, and toss.

Quinoa with Vegetables

Ingredients:

1 cup quinoa
1 cup of diced tomatoes
1/2 cup of diced red onion
2 tablespoons of olive oil
1 tablespoon of lemon juice

Nutritional Information:
(per serving)

Calories: ~350 kcal
Protein: 10 g
Fat: ~20 g
Carbs: ~30 g
Sugar: ~7 g
Fiber: ~8 g

Instructions:

1. Rinse the quinoa, bring to a boil with water and cook for 15-20 minutes. Chop the tomatoes and onions.
2. Mix all the ingredients in a bowl. Add salt and spices to taste.
3. Season with olive oil and lemon juice, mix.

Rice with Chicken and Olives

Ingredients:

1 cup of white or brown rice
2 cubed chicken breasts
1/2 cup of sliced olives
1 cup of chopped tomatoes
2 tablespoons of olive oil

Nutritional Information:
(per serving)

Calories: ~450 kcal
Protein: ~30 g
Fat: ~12 g
Carbs: ~50 g
Sugar: ~7 g
Fiber: ~5 g

Instructions:

1. In a pot, bring water to a boil, add rice, reduce heat, and simmer for 20-25 minutes until cooked.
2. Along with this, in a skillet, heat olive oil and cook the chicken until done (15 minutes).
3. Add tomatoes, and olives, and cook for another 10 minutes. Season with salt and pepper. Mix the chicken with the cooked rice and serve.

Chickpeas with Green Vegetables

Ingredients:

1 cup of canned chickpeas
1 cup of chopped spinach
1/ cup of chopped broccoli
1/2 cup of diced onion
2 tablespoons of olive oil

Nutritional Information:
(per serving)

Calories: ~300 kcal
Protein: ~15 g
Fat: ~10 g
Carbs: ~35 g
Sugar: ~5 g
Fiber: ~8 g

Instructions:

1. Heat olive oil in a pan. Sauté onion until soft for about 5 minutes.
2. Add broccoli and cook until tender for about 10 minutes.
3. Add spinach and chickpeas, and cook until heated through for about 3-5 minutes.
4 Season with salt and pepper. Toss and serve.

Fish with Green Vegetables

Ingredients:

12 oz of fish fillet (cod, seabass)
1 cup of green peas (canned, fresh or frozen)
1/2 cup of chopped spinach
2 tablespoons of olive oil
1 teaspoon of lemon juice and lemon wedges

Nutritional Information:
(per serving)

Calories: ~280 kcal
Protein: ~30 g
Fat: ~10 g
Carbs: ~15 g
Sugar: ~5 g
Fiber: ~5 g

Instructions:

1. Fry the fish in olive oil for 5-7 minutes on each side, season with salt and pepper. Place on a plate.
2. Add the green peas to the pan and cook for 3-5 minutes, until they become softer. Add the spinach and lemon juice. Cook for another 3-5 minutes, until the spinach wilts. Serve the fish with vegetables.

DINNER

(6 PM)

    Dinner in the Mediterranean diet often features a mix of grilled fish and a variety of vegetables, prepared either stewed or roasted. Fish, packed with omega-3 acids, supports heart health, while stewed and roasted vegetables provide essential fiber, vitamins, and antioxidants. These cooking methods enhance the natural flavors of the vegetables, making them both delicious and nutritious. This combination helps maintain stable energy levels, supports digestion, and aligns with the Mediterranean diet's focus on heart-healthy, minimally processed foods, promoting overall well-being and balanced nutrition.

Tilapia with Tomatoes and Olives

Ingredients:
8 oz of tilapia fillets
1 cup of olives
3-4 chopped small tomatoes
1/2 sliced lemon
2 tablespoons of olive oil

Nutritional Information:
(per serving)

Calories: ~280 kcal
Protein: ~30 g
Fat: ~14 g
Carbs: ~10 g
Sugar: ~4 g
Fiber: ~3 g

Instructions:
1. Heat olive oil in a skillet over medium heat and sear tilapia fillets on both sides until golden brown, about 3-5 minutes per side. Remove fish from skillet.
2. In the same skillet, sauté tomatoes and olives for 3-5 minutes, add salt and pepper.
3. Serve fish topped with the tomato and olive sauce with lemon.

Chicken with Olives and Tomatoes

Ingredients:

12 oz of chicken breasts
1 cup of chopped tomatoes
1/4 cup of black olives
1 tablespoon of olive oil
1 teaspoon of oregano

Nutritional Information:
(per serving)

Calories: ~350 kcal
Protein: ~30 g
Fat: ~15 g
Carbs: ~12 g
Sugar: ~4 g
Fiber: ~3 g

Instructions:

1. Heat olive oil in a skillet. Sear chicken until golden brown, for 7-10 minutes per side.
2. Add tomatoes, olives, oregano, salt and pepper. Simmer covered for a more tender dish for 15-20 minutes until chicken is cooked through.

Salmon with Lemon and Green Beans

Ingredients:

12 oz of salmon fillet
1 sliced lemon
1½ cups of fresh green beans
2 minced cloves of garlic
1 tablespoon of olive oil

Instructions:

1. Preheat oven to 180°C (350°F). Place the salmon fillet on a baking sheet, brush with olive oil, add crushed garlic, season with salt and pepper, and top with lemon slices.
2. Bake for 15-20 minutes. Boil the green beans separately until tender (about 5 minutes).
3. Serve the fish with green beans.

Nutritional Information:
(per serving)

Calories: ~350 kcal
Protein: ~30 g
Fat: ~18 g
Carbs: ~10 g
Sugar: ~2 g
Fiber: ~4 g

Stuffed Peppers with Quinoa

Ingredients:
4 medium bell peppers
1 cup of quinoa
1/2 cup of canned beans
1/2 cup of chopped tomatoes
1 tablespoon of olive oil

Nutritional Information:
(per serving)

Calories: ~320 kcal
Protein: ~10 g
Fat: ~8 g
Carbs: ~55 g
Sugar: ~6 g
Fiber: ~9 g

Instructions:

1. Preheat oven to 180°C (350°F). Cut the tops off the peppers and remove the seeds.
2. Cook quinoa according to package instructions (10 minutes). Mix with beans, tomatoes, salt, and pepper.
3. Stuff the peppers with the mixture and bake for 20-25 minutes.

Mushrooms with Garlic and Herbs

Ingredients:

2 cups of mushrooms
3 minced cloves of garlic
2 tablespoons of sour cream
2 tablespoons of olive oil
2 tablespoons of chopped parsley

Nutritional Information:
(per serving)

Calories: ~340 kcal
Protein: ~6 g
Fat: ~35 g
Carbs: ~10 g
Sugar: ~5 g
Fiber: ~3 g

Instructions:

1. Preheat oven to 200°C (400°F). Arrange mushrooms on a baking sheet.
2. Mix sour cream, garlic, olive oil, salt, and pepper. Drizzle over mushrooms and bake for 15-20 minutes.
3. Sprinkle with parsley before serving.

Turkey with Broccoli

Ingredients:

7 oz of ground turkey
1 cup of broccoli
1 cup of diced onion
2 minced garlic cloves
2 tablespoons of olive oil

Nutritional Information:
(per serving)

Calories: ~370 kcal
Protein: ~28 g
Fat: ~24 g
Carbs: ~12 g
Sugar: ~3 g
Fiber: ~4 g

Instructions:

1. Fry the onion, stirring, for about 3-4 min. Add the ground turkey, season with salt and pepper. Cook, stirring, for about 10-12 min. Remove the turkey and onions from the pan and set aside.
2. In the same pan, heat the remaining olive oil and fry the garlic for 1-2 minutes. Add the broccoli and cook for 7-10 minutes.
3. Combine everything and serve.

Fish Cakes

Ingredients:

12 oz of fish fillet (cod, catfish)
2 eggs
1/2 cup of breadcrumbs
1 tablespoon of olive oil
1 lemon for juice and zest

Nutritional Information:
(per serving)

Calories: ~320 kcal
Protein: ~25 g
Fat: ~15 g
Carbs: ~20 g
Sugar: ~2 g
Fiber: ~3 g

Instructions:

1. Blend the fish in a blender. Mix with egg, breadcrumbs, lemon juice and zest, salt, and pepper.
2. Form patties and fry in a skillet with olive oil for 4-6 minutes per side. You can fry it under the lid for softness.
3. Serve with your favorite sauce.

Vegetables Baked with Cheese

Ingredients:
1 cup of diced eggplant
1 cup of diced zucchini
1 cup of diced bell pepper
1/2 cup of grated parmesan cheese
2 tablespoons of olive oil

Nutritional Information:
(per serving)
Calories: ~250 kcal
Protein: ~10 g
Fat: ~15 g
Carbs: ~20 g
Sugar: ~6 g
Fiber: ~6 g

Instructions:
1. Preheat oven to 200°C (400°F). Arrange vegetables on a baking sheet.
2. Mix ½ cup water, and olive oil with salt and pepper. Drizzle over vegetables and bake for 25 minutes. Sprinkle with Parmesan and bake for another 5 minutes.
3. Let it sit to cool and serve warm.

Shrimp in Tomato Sauce

Ingredients:

12 oz of peeled and deveined shrimp
1 cup of crushed tomatoes
2 finely chopped cloves of garlic
1/4 cup of chopped fresh basil
1 tablespoon of olive oil

Nutritional Information:
(per serving)

Calories: ~220 kcal
Protein: ~23 g
Fat: ~8 g
Carbs: ~10 g
Sugar: ~6 g
Fiber: ~2 g

Instructions:

1. Heat olive oil in a skillet over medium heat. Add garlic and sauté until golden for about 1 minute.
2. Add tomatoes, salt, and pepper. Simmer for 5 minutes.
3. Add shrimp and cook for another 7-10 minutes, until they turn pink and are cooked through. Stir in chopped basil and serve hot.

Quinoa with Vegetables and Tahini

Ingredients:

1 cup of quinoa
1 cup of chopped tomatoes
1/2 cup of chopped cucumbers
1/4 cup of tahini
1 tablespoon of olive oil

Nutritional Information:
(per serving)

Calories: ~350 kcal
Protein: ~12 g
Fat: ~18 g
Carbs: ~40 g
Sugar: ~5 g
Fiber: ~6 g

Instructions:

1. Cook quinoa according to package instructions (10-15 minutes).
2. Mix with tomatoes and cucumbers.
3. In a bowl, combine tahini with olive oil, salt, and pepper. Drizzle over and toss.

Cod with Lemon and Capers

Ingredients:

12 oz of fish fillet (cod or seabass)
1 sliced lemon
2 tablespoons of capers
2 tablespoons of olive oil
1 teaspoon of dried thyme

Nutritional Information:
(per serving)

Calories: ~250 kcal
Protein: ~30 g
Fat: ~12 g
Carbs: ~6 g
Sugar: ~1 g
Fiber: ~1 g

Instructions:

1. Preheat the oven to 200°C (400°F). Place the cod fillets on a baking tray.
2. Drizzle the fish with olive oil, and sprinkle with thyme, salt and pepper. Arrange the lemon slices and capers on top.
3. Bake in the oven for 15-20 minutes.

Tuna with Tomatoes and Olives

Ingredients:

12 oz of canned tuna
1 cup of chopped tomatoes
1/2 cup of black olives
1 tablespoon of olive oil
1 teaspoon of oregano

Nutritional Information:
(per serving)

Calories: ~280 kcal
Protein: ~25 g
Fat: ~15 g
Carbs: ~12 g
Sugar: ~5 g
Fiber: ~4 g

Instructions:

1. Heat olive oil in a skillet. Add tomatoes and olives, sauté for 5-7 minutes.
2. Add tuna (no liquid), oregano, salt, and pepper. Cook for an additional 3-5 minutes.

Chicken with Potatoes and Rosemary

Ingredients:

4 chicken drumsticks
6 small potatoes
2 tablespoons of olive oil
2 minced cloves garlic
1 tablespoon of fresh rosemary or a whole sprig

Nutritional Information:
(per serving)

Calories: ~450 kcal
Protein: ~30 g
Fat: ~20 g
Carbs: ~35 g
Sugar: ~2 g
Fiber: ~5 g

Instructions:

1. Preheat oven to 200°C (400°F). Place chicken legs and potatoes on a baking sheet.
2. Mix minced garlic with 1/2 cup water and olive oil. Pour this mixture over your dish, and sprinkle with rosemary, salt, and pepper.
3. Bake for 25-30 minutes until cooked.

Pasta with Spinach and Feta Sauce

Ingredients:

1 cup of whole grain pasta (penne rigate)
2 cups of spinach
1/2 cup of feta
1 tablespoon of olive oil
2 minced cloves of garlic

Nutritional Information:
(per serving)

Calories: ~350 kcal
Protein: ~15 g
Fat: ~14 g
Carbs: ~45 g
Sugar: ~4 g
Fiber: ~6 g

Instructions:

1. Cook pasta according to package instructions (10-15 minutes) and drain water after.
2. Heat olive oil in a skillet and sauté garlic until golden. Add spinach and cook until wilted 3-5 minutes.
3. Mix spinach with pasta and feta. Season with salt and pepper.

Shrimp with Lemon and Herbs

Ingredients:

12 oz of peeled and deveined shrimp
1 small sliced lemon
2 tablespoons of chopped fresh parsley and dill
2 finely chopped cloves of garlic
2 tablespoons of olive oil

Nutritional Information:
(per serving)

Calories: ~300 kcal
Protein: ~40 g
Fat: ~15 g
Carbs: ~5 g
Sugar: ~1 g
Fiber: ~1 g

Instructions:

1. Preheat oven to 200°C (400°F).
2. Place shrimp in a bowl. Add olive oil, lemon and lemon juice, parsley, dill, garlic, salt, and pepper. Toss to fully coat the shrimps.
3. Spread shrimp in a single layer on a baking sheet. Bake for 10-12 minutes, until shrimp are pink and cooked through. Serve hot.

SALADS

   In the Mediterranean diet, salads play a vital role in providing a fresh and nutritious component to meals. Typically, Mediterranean salads are made with a variety of fresh vegetables like tomatoes, cucumbers, and bell peppers, often complemented by olives, herbs, and a drizzle of extra-virgin olive oil. These salads are rich in vitamins, minerals, and antioxidants, supporting overall health and digestion. They also offer a satisfying crunch and can be topped with lean proteins such as grilled chicken or fish for a complete meal. Incorporating salads into daily meals helps maintain heart health, supports weight management, and enhances overall well-being.

Tomato and Mozzarella Salad

Ingredients:

2 medium sliced tomatoes
1 cup of sliced mozzarella cheese
1 tablespoon of olive oil
1 tablespoon of balsamic vinegar
basil leaves for garnish

Nutritional Information:
(per serving)

Calories: ~180 kcal
Protein: ~8 g
Fat: ~14 g
Carbs: ~6 g
Sugar: ~4 g
Fiber: ~2 g

Instructions:

1. Arrange sliced tomatoes and mozzarella on a plate.
2. Drizzle with olive oil and balsamic vinegar, season with salt and pepper.
3. Garnish with basil leaves.

Chicken Apple Walnut Salad

Ingredients:

8 oz of sliced chicken breast
1/4 cup of walnuts
1 cup of diced apples
1/2 cup of diced celery
2 tablespoons yogurt

Nutritional Information:
(per serving)

Calories: ~400 kcal
Protein: ~25 g
Fat: ~20 g
Carbs: ~25 g
Sugar: ~10 g
Fiber: ~5 g

Instructions:

1. Fry the chicken breast in a frying pan with a little olive oil for 20 minutes. Cut into slices.
2. In a bowl, mix the chopped chicken, walnuts, apples and celery.
3. Season with yogurt and mix. Add lemon juice and fresh herbs if desired.

Olive and Cheese Salad

Ingredients:

1 cup of olives
1/2 cup of crumbled feta cheese
1 cup of chopped tomatoes
1/2 cup of chopped red onion
2 tablespoons of olive oil

Nutritional Information:
(per serving)

Calories: ~250 kcal
Protein: ~10 g
Fat: ~19 g
Carbs: ~15 g
Sugar: ~4 g
Fiber: ~4 g

Instructions:

1. Combine all ingredients in a bowl.
2. Drizzle with olive oil and add salt and pepper to taste, toss to cover.

Tuna and Bean Salad

Ingredients:

12 oz of drained tuna
1/2 cup of rinsed and drained canned beans
1 medium chopped cucumber
1/2 cup of chopped red onion
1 tablespoon of olive oil

Nutritional Information:
(per serving)

Calories: ~270 kcal
Protein: ~20 g
Fat: ~8 g
Carbs: ~28 g
Sugar: ~4 g
Fiber: ~8 g

Instructions:

1. Combine all ingredients in a bowl.
2. Drizzle with olive oil, add salt and pepper to taste, and toss to cover.

Broccoli and Carrot Salad

Ingredients:

2 cups of chopped broccoli
1 large grated carrot
1/4 cup of sunflower seeds
1 tablespoon of olive oil
1 tablespoon of lemon juice

Nutritional Information:
(per serving)

Calories: ~160 kcal
Protein: ~5 g
Fat: ~8 g
Carbs: ~20 g
Sugar: ~5 g
Fiber: ~6 g

Instructions:

1. Boil broccoli for 5-7 minutes in boiling water, let cool down a bit, and disassemble into small florets.
2. Combine all ingredients in a bowl.
3. Drizzle with olive oil and lemon juice. Add salt and pepper and mix.

Bean and Corn Salad

Ingredients:

1 can of rinsed and drained canned beans
1/2 cup of canned corn
1 cup of chopped tomatoes
1/2 cup of chopped red onion
1 tablespoon of olive oil

Nutritional Information:
(per serving)

Calories: ~230 kcal
Protein: ~10 g
Fat: ~5 g
Carbs: ~35 g
Sugar: ~6 g
Fiber: ~8 g

Instructions:

1. Combine all ingredients in a bowl.
2. Drizzle with olive oil, and toss to cover.

Chicken and Orange Salad

Ingredients:

8 oz of chicken breast
1 medium sliced orange
1/2 cup of walnuts
1 tablespoon of olive oil
2 tablespoons of balsamic vinegar

Nutritional Information:
(per serving)

Calories: ~290 kcal
Protein: 22 g
Fat: ~16 g
Carbs: ~20 g
Sugar: ~12 g
Fiber: ~5 g

Instructions:

1. Brown the chicken breast in a pan with a little olive oil for 20 minutes. Cut into cubes.
2. Mix all ingredients in a bowl. Add salt and pepper to taste.
3. Drizzle with olive oil and balsamic vinegar and toss to coat.

DESSERTS

In the Mediterranean diet, desserts are enjoyed in moderation and often feature fresh, wholesome ingredients. Common Mediterranean desserts include fruit-based options like fresh berries, citrus fruits, or baked apples. These desserts emphasize natural sweetness and are rich in vitamins, antioxidants, and fiber. Occasionally, you might find traditional sweets like Greek yogurt with honey and nuts or a small serving of fruit sorbet. These choices align with the diet's focus on minimal processing and healthy ingredients, offering a satisfying end to a meal while supporting overall health and wellness. The emphasis is on enjoying sweets as a small, balanced part of a nutritious lifestyle.

Coconut Balls

Ingredients:

1/2 cup of shredded coconut
1/2 cup of cottage cheese
1/2 cup of almond butter
2 tablespoons of honey
2 tablespoons of caramel

Nutritional Information:
(per serving)

Calories: ~180 kcal
Protein: ~12 g
Fat: ~16 g
Carbs: ~15 g
Sugar: ~8 g
Fiber: ~3 g

Instructions:

1. Mix all ingredients and form small balls. Roll the finished balls in coconut flakes.
2. Chill in the refrigerator. Let stand for 15-20 minutes.
3. Drizzle with caramel.

Apples with Nuts and Cinnamon

Ingredients:

2 large apples
1/2 cup of chopped walnuts
2 tablespoons of honey
1 teaspoon of cinnamon
1/2 cup of raisins

Nutritional Information:
(per serving)

Calories: ~180 kcal
Protein: ~2 g
Fat: ~5 g
Carbs: ~35 g
Sugar: ~26 g
Fiber: ~6 g

Instructions:

1. **Preheat oven to 350°F (180°C).**
2. **Core the apples and place them in a baking dish.**
3. **Mix walnuts, honey, cinnamon, and raisins in a bowl. Stuff the apples with the mixture.**
4. **Bake for 25-30 minutes until apples are tender.**

Cottage Cheese Pancakes with Honey

Ingredients:

1 cup of cottage cheese
1 egg
1/2 cup of whole grain flour
1/2 cup of milk
2 tablespoons of honey

Nutritional Information:
(per serving)

Calories: ~220 kcal
Protein: ~15 g
Fat: ~8 g
Carbs: ~25 g
Sugar: ~12 g
Fiber: ~3 g

Instructions:

1. Mix all ingredients until smooth.
2. Cook pancakes on a heated skillet until golden brown on both sides.

Grapes with Honey and Nuts

Ingredients:

2 cups of grapes (green or red)
2 tablespoons of honey
1/4 cup of chopped walnuts
1 teaspoon of cinnamon
1 teaspoon of lemon juice

Nutritional Information:
(per serving)

Calories: ~120 kcal
Protein: ~2 g
Fat: ~4 g
Carbs: ~20 g
Sugar: ~15 g
Fiber: ~2 g

Instructions:

1. Preheat oven to 350°F (180°C).
2. Place grapes in a baking dish. Drizzle with honey, and lemon juice, and sprinkle with walnuts and cinnamon.
3. Bake for 15-20 minutes until grapes are tender. Serve warm.

Almond Cookies

Ingredients:

1 cup of almond flour
1/4 cup of honey
1/4 cup of coconut oil
1 egg
1/2 cup of milk

Nutritional Information:
(per serving)

Calories: ~150 kcal
Protein: ~5 g
Fat: ~12 g
Carbs: ~10 g
Sugar: ~8 g
Fiber: ~2 g

Instructions:

1. Mix all ingredients and form small cookies.
2. Bake at 180°C (350°F) for 10-15 minutes.

Fruit Salad with Honey and Nuts

Ingredients:

1 large apple
1 large pear
1 cup of grapes
1/2 cup of nuts (walnuts, almonds)
2 tablespoons of honey

Nutritional Information:
(per serving)

Calories: ~280 kcal
Protein: ~4 g
Fat: ~12 g
Carbs: ~40 g
Sugar: ~28 g
Fiber: ~7 g

Instructions:

1. Dice the apple and pear.
2. Mix them with grapes and nuts.
3. Drizzle with honey, and toss to cover.

Pears with Nuts and Feta

Ingredients:

2 large halved and cored pears
1/4 cup of chopped nuts (walnuts or almonds)
1/2 cup of feta cheese
2 tablespoons of honey
1/2 teaspoon of cinnamon

Nutritional Information:
(per serving)

Calories: ~200 kcal
Protein: ~3 g
Fat: ~10 g
Carbs: ~30 g
Sugar: ~25 g
Fiber: ~5 g

Instructions:

1. Place pears on a baking sheet, sprinkle with nuts and drizzle with honey.
2. Bake at 180°C (350°F) for 15-20 minutes. Sprinkle with feta cheese before serving.

BEVERAGES

In the Mediterranean diet, beverages are integral to a healthy lifestyle. Water is the primary drink, crucial for hydration and overall well-being. Herbal teas, such as mint or chamomile, are also popular for their soothing and health-promoting properties. Moderate consumption of red wine with meals is traditional, offering potential heart health benefits due to its antioxidants, but should be enjoyed responsibly. Fresh fruit juices, preferably without added sugars, provide a nutritious and refreshing option. The focus is on natural, minimally processed drinks that support hydration and complement a balanced diet, enhancing overall health and vitality.

Lemon Water with Mint

Nutritional Information (per serving)
Calories: 10 kcal | Protein: 0 g | Fat: 0 g | Carbs: 2 g | Sugar: 2 g | Fiber: 0 g

Ingredients
1 medium sliced lemon | fresh mint leaves | 4 cups of water

Instructions
1. Add lemon slices and mint to the water.
2. Refrigerate for 1-2 hours

Nutritional Information (per serving)
Calories: 180 kcal | Protein: 7 g | Fat: 2 g | Carbs: 35 g | Sugar: 25 g | Fiber: 4 g

Ingredients
2 medium apples | 1 cup of Greek yogurt | 1 cup of apple juice | 1/2 of teaspoon cinnamon

Instructions
1. Blend all ingredients until smooth.

Apple Cinnamon Smoothie

Watermelon Mint Cocktail

Nutritional Information (per serving**)**
Calories: 90 kcal| Protein: 1 g | Fat: 0 g | Carbs: 23 g | Sugar: 19 g | Fiber: 1 g

Ingredients
2 cups of watermelon cubes | mint leaves | 2 tablespoons of lemon juice

Instructions
1. Blend watermelon, mint, and lemon juice until smooth.

Nutritional Information (per serving)
Calories: 60 kcal | Protein: 2 g | Fat: 1 g | Carbos: 10 g | Sugar: 4 g | Fiber: 1 g

Ingredients
2 cups of black coffee | 1/2 cup of oat milk | 1 teaspoon of cinnamon

Instructions
1. Brew the black coffee.
2. Heat the oat milk and add it to the coffee. Sprinkle cinnamon on top and stir.

Coffee with Oat milk and Cinnamon

Apple and Kefir Smoothie

Nutritional Information (per serving)
Calories: 220 kcal | Protein: 6 g | Fat: 3 g | Carbs: 40 g | Sugar: 25 g | Fiber: 5 g

Ingredients
2 medium apples | 2 cups of kefir | 2 tablespoons of honey

Instructions
1. Place all ingredients in a blender and blend until smooth.

Nutritional Information (per serving)
Calories: 45 kcal | Protein: 1 g | Fat: 0 g | Carbos: 11 g | Sugar: 8 g | Fiber: 1 g

Ingredients
2 teaspoons of turmeric powder | juice from 2 oranges | 2 teaspoons of honey | 2 cups of hot water

Instructions
1. In a cup, mix turmeric powder with hot water until well combined.
2. Add orange juice and honey, and stir.

Orange Turmeric Tea

Blueberry Apple Cocktail

Nutritional Information (per serving)
Calories: 120 kcal | Protein: 1 g | Fat: 0 g | Carbs: 30 g | Sugar: 22 g | Fiber: 4 g

Ingredients
2 medium apples | 1 cup of water | 1 cup of apple juice | 1 cup of blueberries

Instructions
1. Blend all ingredients until smooth.

Nutritional Information (per serving)
Calories: 110 kcal | Protein: 2 g | Fat: 0 g | Carbs: 26 g | Sugar: 21 g | Fiber: 1 g

Ingredients
2 cups of fresh orange juice | 1 teaspoon of grated ginger

Instructions
1. Mix juice and ginger.

Orange Ginger Cocktail

Oat Milk with Honey and Vanilla

Nutritional Information (per serving)
Calories: 120 kcal | Protein: 2 g | Fat: 2 g | Carbs: 24 g | Sugar: 16 g | Fiber: 1 g

Ingredients
2 cups of oat milk | 2 tablespoons of honey | 1/2 teaspoon of vanilla extract

Instructions
1. Mix all ingredients together and stir well.

Nutritional Information (per serving)
Calories: 50 kcal | Protein: 1 g | Fat: 0 g | Carbs: 12 g | Sugar: 10 g | Fiber: 1 g

Ingredients
1 medium cucumber | 1 cup of fresh lime juice | 2 cups of water | 1 tablespoon of honey

Instructions
1. Blend cucumber with lime juice and water. Strain if needed.

Cucumber Lime Cooler

Cold Green Tea with Cucumber

Nutritional Information (per serving)
Calories: 5 kcal | Protein: 0 g | Fat: 0 g | Carbs: 1 g | Sugar: 0 g | Fiber: 0 g

Ingredients
2 green tea bags | 1 medium sliced cucumber | 2 cups of hot water | ice

Instructions
1. Brew the green tea bag in hot water for 2-3 minutes.
2. Chill the tea and add the sliced cucumber. Serve over ice.

Nutritional Information (per serving)
Calories: 40 kcal | Protein: 0 g | Fat: 0 g | Carbs: 10 g | Sugar: 10 g | Fiber: 0 g

Ingredients
2 chamomile tea bags | 1 cup of apple juice | 2 cups of hot water

Instructions
1. Brew the chamomile tea bag in hot water for 5 minutes.
2. Add apple juice and stir.

Chamomile tea with Apple juice

Strawberry Lemonade

Nutritional Information (per serving)
Calories: 80 kcal | Protein: 0 g | Fat: 0 g | Carbs: 21 g | Sugar: 18 g | Fiber: 1 g

Ingredients
2 cups of fresh strawberries | 1 cup of lemon juice | 2 cups of water | 1-2 tablespoons of honey

Instructions
1. Blend strawberries into a puree.
2. Mix puree with lemon juice, water, and honey. Stir well.

Nutritional Information (per serving)
Calories: 200 kcal | Protein: 1 g | Fat: 6 g | Carbs: 36 g | Sugar: 30 g | Fiber: 2 g

Ingredients
1 cup of coconut milk | 1 cup of chopped mango | 1 cup of chopped pineapple

Instructions
1. Blend all ingredients until smooth.

Pineapple Mango Smoothie

 SHOPPING LIST

I know that all of us have a busy schedule, and grocery shopping can often be a time-consuming task. That's why I've put together a comprehensive shopping list of your new dishes to make your life easier. In addition, as a special bonus, my a list of products from Amazon USA, so you can shop conveniently from home in one to two clicks.

And now you have everything you need to follow your 4(+)-week meal plan (you can find it further). Access this exclusive bonus through the QR code provided below.

SPECIAL BONUS IS HERE

Our life is fast and fleeting. But it is beautiful! The main concept of my longevity book is not to become a hostage to your kitchen and the long processes around it. If you are interested in the speed and benefit of the time spent on the process of nutrition, I suggest you take advantage of my **second special digital bonus** with an interactive shopping list. **Don't worry, your private data will be safe!**

To collect a bonus, **simply scan this QR code with your smartphone** to get access immediately and without any obligations! Well, let's continue...

 WEEK MEAL PLAN

In this book, I offer a 4-week meal plan with recipes designed to help you reach your weight loss goals and improve your overall health. By following the plan, you'll enjoy healthy foods and develop sustainable eating habits for long-term success. Whether you want to lose weight or eat better, this plan will help you feel better in the future.

It includes page numbers that take you directly to the recipes you'll need every day. This makes it easy to find and prepare meals, ensuring you stay organized and on track throughout your journey. The meal plan can be found further on pages 81-82.

BREAKFASTS	LUNCH	DINNER	SALADS	DESSERTS	BEVERAGES	WEEK
#9 Muesli with Almond Milk and Fruit	#25 Fish with Garlic and Brussel Sprouts	#41 Tilapia with Tomatoes and Olives	#57 Tomato and Mozzarella Salad	#65 Coconut Balls	#73 Lemon Water with Mint	
#10 Whole Grain Toast with Tomatoes	#26 Chickpea Soup with Tomatoes	#42 Chicken with Olives and Tomatoes	#58 Chicken Apple Walnut Salad	#66 Apples with Nuts and Cinnamon	#73 Apple Cinnamon Smoothie	
#11 Oatmeal with Berries and Almonds	#27 Pasta with Tomato Olive Sauce	#43 Salmon with Lemon and Green Beans	#59 Olive and Cheese Salad	#67 Cottage Cheese Pancakes with Honey	#74 Watermelon Mint Cocktail	1 week
#12 Greek Yogurt with Fruit and Chia Seeds	#28 Vegetable Stew	#44 Stuffed Peppers with Quinoa	#60 Tuna and Bean Salad	#68 Grapes with Honey and Nuts	#74 Coffee with Oat milk and Cinnamon	
#13 Spinach and Tomato Omelet	#29 Rice with Vegetables and Feta	#45 Mushrooms with Garlic and Herbs	#61 Broccoli and Carrot Salad	#69 Almond Cookies	#75 Apple and Kefir Smoothie	
#14 Whole Grain Pancakes with Honey	#30 Tomato Basil Soup	#46 Turkey with Broccoli	#62 Bean and Corn Salad	#70 Fruit Salad with Honey and Nuts	#75 Orange Turmeric Tea	
#15 Avocado Toast with Poached Egg	#31 Pasta with Mushrooms and Parmesan	#47 Fish Cakes	#63 Chicken and Orange Salad	#71 Pears with Nuts and Feta	#76 Blueberry Apple Cocktail	
#16 Oatmeal with Kiwi and Chia Seeds	#32 Chicken Vegetable Rice	#48 Vegetables Baked with Cheese	#61 Broccoli and Carrot Salad	#66 Apples with Nuts and Cinnamon	#76 Orange Ginger Cocktail	
#17 Bruschetta with Tomatoes and Basil	#33 Salmon with Broccolis	#49 Shrimp in Tomato Sauce	#57 Tomato and Mozzarella Salad	#70 Fruit Salad with Honey and Nuts	#77 Oat Milk with Honey and Vanilla	
#18 Eggs with Avocado and Tomatoes	#34 Lavash with Hummus and Vegetables	#50 Quinoa with Vegetables and Tahini	#60 Tuna and Bean Salad	#69 Almond Cookies	#77 Cucumber Lime Cooler	2 week
#19 Quinoa with Nuts and Honey	#35 Boiled Potatoes with Green Beans	#51 Cod with Lemon and Capers	#61 Broccoli and Carrot Salad	#67 Cottage Cheese Pancakes with Honey	#78 Cold Green Tea with Cucumber	
#20 Tuna and Avocado Toast	#36 Quinoa with Vegetables	#52 Tuna with Tomatoes and Olives	#62 Bean and Corn Salad	#65 Coconut Balls	#78 Chamomile tea with Apple juice	
#21 Vegetable and Feta Cheese Frittata	#37 Rice with Chicken and Olives	#53 Chicken with Potatoes and Rosemary	#59 Olive and Cheese Salad	#68 Grapes with Honey and Nuts	#79 Strawberry Lemonade	
#22 Toast with Hummus and Vegetables	#38 Chickpeas with Green Vegetables	#54 Pasta with Spinach and Feta Sauce	#58 Chicken Apple Walnut Salad	#71 Pears with Nuts and Feta	#79 Pineapple Mango Smoothie	

WEEK	BREAKFASTS	LUNCH	DINNER	SALADS	DESSERTS	BEVERAGES
3 week	#23 Broccoli and Parmesan Omelet	#39 Fish with Green Vegetables	#55 Shrimp with Lemon and Herbs	#59 Olive and Cheese Salad	#69 Almond Cookies	#73 Apple Cinnamon Smoothie
	#14 Whole Grain Pancakes with Honey	#30 Tomato Basil Soup	#50 Quinoa with Vegetables and Tahini	#63 Chicken and Orange Salad	#68 Grapes with Honey and Nuts	#74 Coffee with Oat milk and Cinnamon
	#21 Vegetable and Feta Cheese Frittata	#35 Boiled Potatoes with Green Beans	#43 Salmon with Lemon and Green beans	#61 Broccoli and Carrot Salad	#65 Coconut Balls	#75 Orange Turmeric Tea
	#10 Whole Grain Toast with Tomatoes	#31 Pasta with Mushrooms and Parmesan	#48 Vegetables Baked with Cheese	#60 Tuna and Bean Salad	#70 Fruit Salad with Honey and Nuts	#76 Orange Ginger Cocktail
	#23 Broccoli and Parmesan Omelet	#28 Vegetable Stew	#53 Chicken with Potatoes and Rosemary	#62 Bean and Corn Salad	#71 Pears with Nuts and Feta	#77 Cucumber Lime Cooler
	#11 Oatmeal with Berries and Almonds	#34 Lavash with Hummus and Vegetables	#42 Chicken with Olives and Tomatoes	#57 Tomato and Mozzarella Salad	#67 Cottage Cheese Pancakes with Honey	#78 Chamomile tea with Apple juice
	#18 Eggs with Avocado and Tomatoes	#38 Chickpeas with Green Vegetables	#55 Shrimp with Lemon and Herbs	#58 Chicken Apple Walnut Salad	#71 Pears with Nuts and Feta	#79 Pineapple Mango Smoothie
4 week	#16 Oatmeal with Kiwi and Chia Seeds	#37 Rice with Chicken and Olives	#41 Tilapia with Tomatoes and Olives	#63 Chicken and Orange Salad	#69 Almond Cookies	#73 Lemon Water with Mint
	#20 Tuna and Avocado Toast	#26 Chickpea Soup with Tomatoes	#52 Tuna with Tomatoes and Olives	#59 Olive and Cheese Salad	#68 Grapes with Honey and Nuts	#74 Watermelon Mint Cocktail
	#22 Toast with Hummus and Vegetables	#33 Salmon with Broccolis	#45 Mushrooms with Garlic and Herbs	#59 Olive and Cheese Salad	#70 Fruit Salad with Honey and Nuts	#75 Apple and Kefir Smoothie
	#17 Bruschetta with Tomatoes and Basil	#39 Fish with Green Vegetables	#51 Cod with Lemon and Capers	#58 Chicken Apple Walnut Salad	#66 Apples with Nuts and Cinnamon	#76 Blueberry Apple Cocktail
	#9 Muesli with Almond Milk and Fruit	#27 Pasta with Tomato Olive Sauce	#47 Fish Cakes	#60 Tuna and Bean Salad	#65 Coconut Balls	#77 Oat Milk with Honey and Vanilla
	#12 Greek Yogurt with Fruit and Chia Seeds	#36 Quinoa with Vegetables	#44 Stuffed Peppers with Quinoa	#62 Bean and Corn Salad	#71 Pears with Nuts and Feta	#78 Cold Green Tea with Cucumber
	#13 Spinach and Tomato Omelet	#25 Fish with Garlic and Brussel sprouts	#54 Pasta with Spinach and Feta Sauce	#57 Tomato and Mozzarella Salad	#67 Cottage Cheese Pancakes with Honey	#79 Strawberry Lemonade

WEIGHT MANAGEMENT

Here you can track your weight over 4 weeks while following our meal plan. You'll be able to monitor your progress, your weight will go down, and your well-being will improve. You will control this process easily and smoothly.

It is easy to use this scheme: In each circle, you write your weight for each new day. There is no need to force anything. Your path to health and longevity should be comfortable and natural. It is good and desirable to combine the diet plan with moderate exercise.

For starters, my advice to you is to start with fresh air walks and RELAX-style exercises. I will talk about some of the exercises on the next page. Try to keep a regular eating and sleeping schedule. Especially focus on getting enough sleep, about 8 hours, as your body will need energy during the initial phase (up to 21 days), as well as discipline and control to develop healthy habits and a subconscious need to stick to them in the future.

LET'S STAY IN TOUCH

I'm used to giving more than is expected of me. For this reason, I offer everyone to familiarize themselves with the basic and minimum set of physical exercises, which, in combination with the 4-week meal plan proposed by me, will have a greater effect in the short term. This is the third of my special bonus for you. Access this exclusive bonus you can through the QR code provided down.

SPECIAL BONUS IS HERE

Regular physical exercise is a key component of the Mediterranean lifestyle. Activities like walking, swimming, or cycling contribute to overall health and well-being. If you are interested in a new complect regular physical exercise by Olivia Efso, as an addition to this diet book, I suggest you take my **third and last special digital bonus**. **Don't worry, your private data will be safe!**

To collect a bonus, **simply scan this QR code with your smartphone** to get access immediately and without any obligations!

As you finish this book, I hope you've discovered not just new recipes, but new experiences in the kitchen. As soon as you try to do it, please let me know how you like it! I welcome all feedback, so please do not be shy and leave your reviews on the page of my book on Amazon where you purchased it! It would mean a lot to me if you could leave a quick review with a video or picture of the masterpieces that you made with the help of this book.

Cooking is an art, a way to express love, creativity, and care for yourself and those around you. Every dish you prepare is a step towards a healthier, happier life. Remember, the recipes here are just the beginning. Feel free to experiment, adapt, and make them your own. The kitchen is your canvas, and you are the artist, let these meals bring joy to your table and warmth to your heart.

Thank you for allowing me to be part of your culinary journey. I hope this book becomes a well-loved companion in your kitchen, inspiring you to create delicious memories for years to come. Let's stay in touch and continue exploring the world of flavors together.

Happy cooking! See you! To be continued...

Yours, Olivia Efso